Simon's Cat®

Simon's Cat ® vs THE WORLD

Simon Tofield

CANONGATE

Edinburgh · London

Published in Great Britain in 2012 by Canongate Books Ltd,
14 High Street, Edinburgh EH1 1TE

www.canongate.tv

1

Copyright © Simon Tofield, 2012

The moral right of the author has been asserted

British Library Cataloguing-in-Publication Data
A catalogue record for this book is available on
request from the British Library

ISBN 978 0 85786 080 4

Typeset by Simon's Cat

Printed and bound in Italy by L.E.G.O. S.p.A.

For my Zoë

... the bird box

...curiosity

... Camping

... walkies

...the vet

... grooming

. . . Roxie

... Monday

... Zebra

... tinned food

... the hornets' nest

. . . barbeque

... Oscar

... the mirror

... kitten control

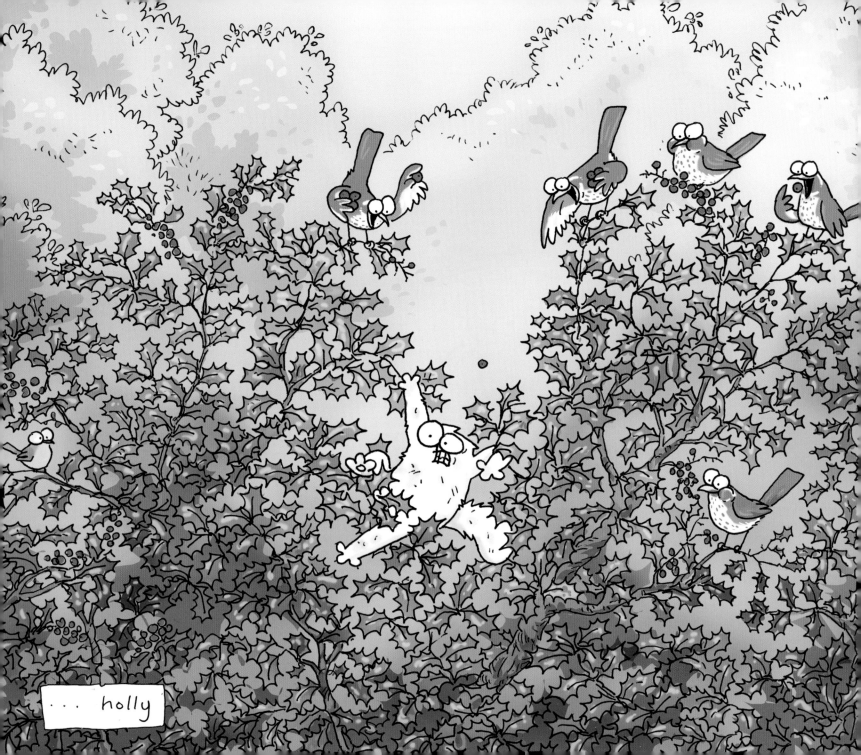

... holly

... sharing

... house work

... garden pond

... novelty hats

... art

... the slide

... Tuesday

... Yoga

... dovecote

... the avalanche

... play time

. . . Foxy

... farm mice

... static

... the fridge

... hedgehog

... the sofa

... Wednesday

... the trampoline

... the cat show

... the woodpecker

... magpie

... Cat nap

... kitten

...the lock in

... catflap

... Squirrel

... Thursday

...HMS Victory

... chickens

... the bike ride

... dinner time

. . . starlings

...Gnome

... Friday

. . . the garden fork

... Water Snake

... the beanbag

... the wheelie bin

... the rabbit patch

... football

... the ants' nest

... the fan

... HD TV

... the clothesline

... Catnip

...the fish tank

. . . Winter

. . . boredom

... the greenhouse

... Saturday afternoon

... bedtime

... Autumn

... Scrabble

. . . bird watching

... public affection

. . . neighbour

... gravity

... Godzilla

... hedgehog revenge

... Pug

... wheatfield

... hibernation

... snow balls

... the kitchen window

... the lawnmower

... the cat basket

... Lenny

... Shower

... fireworks

... Sunday night

Acknowledgements

Thanks to: Zoë Herbert-Jackson, Chris Gavin, Mike Cook, Elena
Turtas, Jon Dunleavy, Filipe Alcada, Tom Bristow, Olly Wilks, Nigel Pay,
Daniel Greaves, Mike Bell. Robert Kirby and Duncan Hayes at UA. Nick
Davies and the Canongate team. Everyone at Stray Cay Rescue
and my cats Maisy, Jess, Hugh and Teddy.

www.Simonscat.com

Simon Tofield is an award-winning animator and cartoonist, who has always expressed himself through drawing. He has had a lifelong interest in animals, beginning as a child, when his uncle gave him a plastic pond which quickly filled with wildlife. Simon was given his first cat when he was nine and now has four rescue cats, who are the mischievous inspiration for his work.